MINISTRY OF PUBLIC BUILDING AND WORKS

The Tower of London

Ministry of Public Building and Works Guide-book

LONDON
HER MAJESTY'S STATIONERY OFFICE
1967 : Reprinted 1969

The Bell Tower (right) with the Byward Tower in the background

The Tower of London

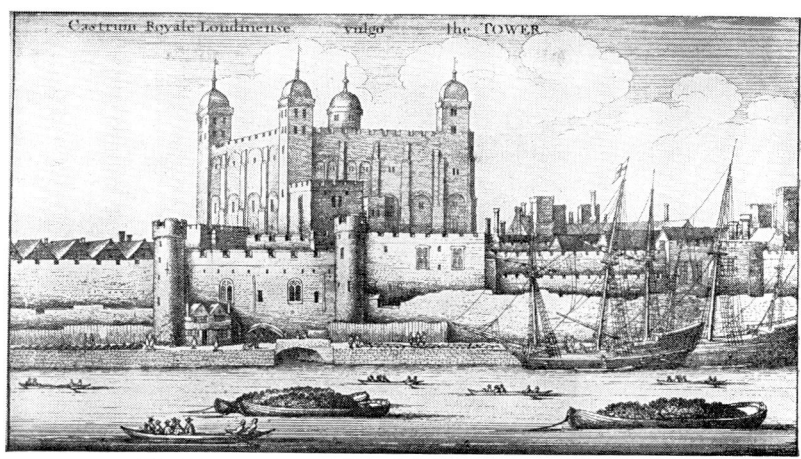

The Tower of London from an engraving by Hollar

THE TOWER OF LONDON was first built by William the Conqueror, for the purpose of protecting and controlling the city. As first planned, it lay within the Roman city walls, but its enlargement in the thirteenth century carried its boundaries eastwards beyond the walls. Nowadays it is wholly within the borough of Tower Hamlets. Including the moat, it covers an area of 18 acres.

Of the present buildings only the White Tower is of the Norman period; but architecture of almost all the styles which have flourished in England may be found within the walls. The Tower has in the past been a fortress, a palace and a prison, and has housed the Royal Mint, the Public Records and (for a short time) the Royal Observatory. It was for centuries the arsenal for small-arms and, being one of the strongest fortresses in the land, the Tower has always guarded the Crown Jewels. From the thirteenth century until 1834 it also housed the Royal Menagerie, the predecessor of the London Zoo.

The oldest and most important building is the Great Tower or Keep, called the White Tower. The Inner Ward is defended by a wall containing thirteen towers, the only surviving original entrance to it being that on the south side under the Bloody Tower. The Outer Ward is defended by a second wall, flanked by six towers on the river face, and by two semicircular

The Tower of London from the river

bastions at the north-west and north-east. A Ditch or Moat, now dry, encircles the whole; it is crossed at the south-western angle by a stone bridge, formerly the drawbridge, leading to the Byward Tower from the Middle Tower, where there was another drawbridge. In front of this was an outwork called the Lion Tower, also surrounded by a moat, which was crossed by a stone causeway, exposed to view in 1936-37. This causeway included a third drawbridge.

The Tower was occupied as a palace by all our Kings and Queens down to James I. It was the custom for each monarch to lodge in the Tower before his coronation, and to ride in procession to Westminster through the city. The Palace buildings stood between the White Tower and the Inner Wall eastward of the Bloody Tower.

Throughout its history the Tower has also been used as the principal place of confinement for State prisoners, from Ralf Flambard in the early twelfth century to Roger Casement (April-May, 1916) and Hitler's deputy, Rudolf Hess (May, 1941), in the twentieth, as well as other historic personages named in later paragraphs of this guide.

Tower Hill

On leaving Tower Hill underground railway station the visitor should cross Trinity square to have an excellent view of the great fortress. Within the railed space of Trinity square the first permanent scaffold on Tower Hill was set up in the reign of Edward IV in 1465, but the first execution recorded here was that of Sir Simon Burley in 1388. Here also were beheaded, among others, Dudley, the minister of Henry VII (1510), his son the Duke of Northumberland (1553), his grandson Lord Guildford Dudley (1554), Thomas Cromwell, Earl of Essex (1540), More and Fisher (1535), Surrey (1547) and his son Norfolk (1572), Strafford (1641) and Archbishop Laud (1645), and the Scottish Lords in 1716, 1746, and 1747, the last being Simon, Lord Lovat.

Passing down the east side of the Tower, one sees the Tower Moat. It was drained in 1843, and part of it is now used as a training and recreation ground. On January 7th, 1928, at 1.30 a.m., a tidal wave swept over the wharf, destroying portions of the retaining walls of the Moat, filling it completely and flooding the Byward Tower to a depth of four feet. As we approach the entrance, we have a good view of the fortifications. On the left is Legge's Mount. To the right is the entrance gateway. The highest building behind is the White Tower, easily distinguished by its four turrets. In front of it are the Devereux, Beauchamp, and Bell Towers, the residences of the Governor and of the Yeoman Gaoler being in the gabled and red-tiled houses between the last two. From one of these windows Lady Jane Grey saw her husband's headless body brought in from Tower Hill.

The Royal Menagerie in the Lion Tower in 1779

The Byward Tower in the days when the moat contained water and (right) today

Queen Elizabeth I, before her accession, was imprisoned in the Tower by her sister Mary, who feared her influence with the Protestants. She is said to have used this part of the walls for exercise, and to this day the ramparts between the Beauchamp Tower and the Bell Tower are known as Elizabeth's Walk.

The Entrance

The modern entrance to the Tower, completed in 1966, passes over the stone causeway which was the only way into the Tower by land in the Middle Ages. This causeway was built by Edward I (1278) and crossed the Outer Moat to the Lion Tower. It had a drawbridge at its outer end, where stood the Lion Gate, and the pit of this drawbridge and the curved slots for its counterweights should be noticed. The Outer Moat was filled up in the latter part of the seventeenth century, and the causeway was buried. It was rediscovered in 1936, and is now exposed to view.

The Lion Tower

The Lion Tower was a wide semicircle, which stood where the ticket office and refreshment room are now. Part of the line of curved outer wall is marked in the roadway. From the thirteenth century to 1834 the Royal Menagerie was lodged within and near it. Another short causeway, still buried on its south side, leads to

The Middle Tower

This also was originally built by Edward I, but it was largely rebuilt in the early eighteenth century. In front of it was the second drawbridge, and the arch under the north side of the causeway let water from the Inner Moat into the drawbridge pit, which exists under the road. Beyond the Middle Tower is the Inner Moat, crossed by another causeway where there was a third drawbridge.

The Byward Tower

This gatehouse of the Outer Ward is the main entrance through the outer circuit of walls. It was built at the end of the thirteenth century, with additions of the time of Richard II. The timber superstructure on the inside was rebuilt in the early sixteenth century. The portcullis with the machinery for raising and lowering it can be seen on the first floor. On either side of the archway are guardrooms with vaulted stone roofs and hooded fireplaces. Part of a fourteenth-century wall-painting, which includes the figures of St. John the Baptist and St. Michael depicted against a background decorated with the leopards of England and fleurs-de-lis of France, has been uncovered in the principal room over the gate passage.

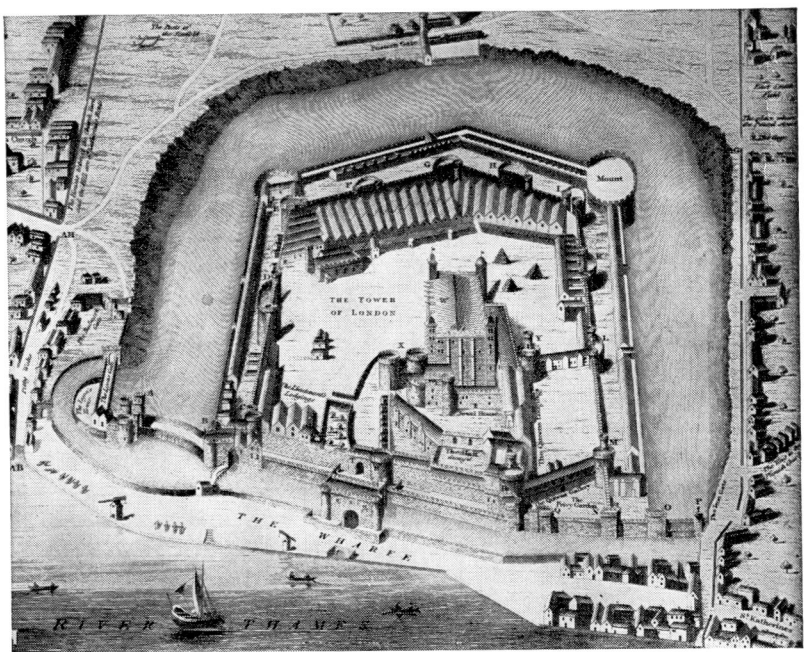

The Tower of London from an engraving based on a survey of 1597

Traitor's Gate beneath St. Thomas's Tower

The Bell Tower

This was planned probably in the reign of Richard I, though its earliest details point to a date early in the thirteenth century. Here Fisher, Bishop of Rochester, St. Thomas More, the Princess Elizabeth, and James, Duke of Monmouth, were confined. The Curtain Wall east of this tower is pierced by the windows of the Lieutenant's Lodgings, now called the Queen's House, and one of these windows lights the Council Chamber, where Guy Fawkes and his fellow conspirators were examined by the Council in 1605 before their public trial at Westminster.

The Traitors' Gate

On the right is now St. Thomas's Tower, with the Traitors' Gate beneath: the wide span of the arch should be noticed. This gate, when the Thames was more of a highway that it is at present, was often used as an entrance to the Tower. In later times it was found convenient as a landing-place for prisoners who had been tried at Westminster. Here successively Edward, Duke of Buckingham (1521), St. Thomas More, Queen Anne Boleyn (1536), Cromwell, Earl of Essex, Queen Katharine Howard (1542), Seymour, Duke of Somerset (1551), Lady Jane Grey (1553), the Princess Elizabeth, Devereux, Earl of Essex (1601), and James, Duke of Monmouth (1685), passed under the arch on their way to prison or the scaffold. St. Thomas's Tower was built by Edward I, and contains a small chapel or oratory dedicated to St. Thomas of Canterbury.

Portion of a mural painting of the fourteenth century discovered in the Byward Tower in 1953

The Bloody Tower

The gateway was built by Henry III and the tower was added over it in the reign of Richard II. It was called by its present name as early as 1597, being believed to be the scene of the murder of Edward V and his brother, the Duke of York. It was originally known as the Garden Tower, as it gives upon that part of the open space which was formerly the Constable's garden. Here Sir Walter Raleigh, whose portrait hangs over the fireplace, was allowed to walk at one time during the twelve years' imprisonment that followed the abortive attempt, at the end of 1603, to place James I's crown on the head of Lady Arabella Stuart. Most of that time Raleigh was detained in the Bloody Tower. His rooms, we are told, were not uncomfortably furnished, his wife and son could visit him, and he had two servants.

In 1616 the King released Raleigh for a fresh expedition to the West Indies; but although he was no doubt hoping for the lion's share of the spoils, James also warned the Spaniards. Continual disaster overtook the expedition, and in August, 1618, Raleigh was once again lodged in the Tower. This time, the King meant to be rid of him. And, on the ground that Raleigh's former sentence still held good, he was beheaded on October 29th in Old Palace Yard, Westminster.

Other prominent occupants of this tower were Laud, Judge Jeffreys, and possibly Monmouth. The interior is furnished with oak furniture from the collection of Sir William Burrell, lent by the Corporation of the

Portcullis mechanism in the Bloody Tower

City of Glasgow. The four-poster bed, dated 1675, comes from the Manor House, Mancetter, Warwickshire, the home of Robert Glover, a Protestant martyr.

Immediately joining this tower on the east is

The Wakefield Tower

The work now to be seen points to its having been built by Henry III. The Great Hall, memorable as the scene of Anne Boleyn's trial, adjoined it, but was pulled down during the Commonwealth. In 1360 the records of the kingdom, which had previously been kept in the White Tower, were lodged here, and this is called in ancient surveys sometimes the Record Tower, sometimes the Hall Tower. The present name is probably derived from William de Wakefield, King's Clerk, appointed to hold custody of the Exchanges in the Tower in 1344. The Tower has two floors; the ground floor acted as a guard room to the thirteenth-century postern which once led to the Royal Apartments. The remains of this small water-gate, which lay immediately against the east side of the Wakefield Tower and a part of Henry III's curtain running eastwards, were revealed in 1957. The upper floor of the Wakefield Tower contains a single vaulted chamber of some magnificence. Under Edward I, a bridge gave access from St. Thomas's

The Royal Mint within the Tower in the eighteenth century

Tower to the Palace via the doorway in the south side of this chamber. The present bridge is a nineteenth-century reconstruction, but the original doorways at either end survive.

The Wall of the Inmost Ward

Running north from the Wakefield Tower is a length of wall built by Henry III. This formed part of the western side of the Inmost Ward, and is pierced with loopholes, each loophole being set in an arched recess on the inner or eastern face of the wall. At its north end it terminated level with the White Tower, and at this point was situated the Coldharbour Tower, which was the main gateway into the Inmost Ward, and is now destroyed. The foundations of the rounded fronts of its two towers have recently been exposed. This length of wall and the foundations of the gateway-towers were for long embedded in a modern building known as the Main Guard. This was destroyed by enemy bombs on December 29th, 1940, and the medieval wall has been carefully cleared of the ruins.

The Crown Jewels

Most of the magnificent regalia displayed date from the seventeenth century. Nearly all the regalia of six centuries of the English monarchy

The Sovereign's Orb

St. Edward's Crown

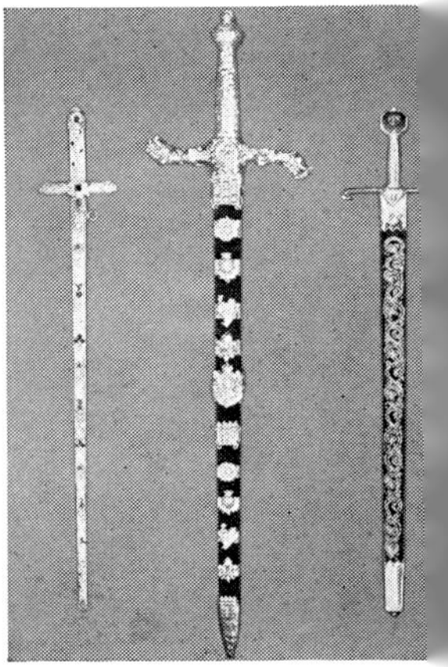

The Swords of State

were sold or melted down by Oliver Cromwell. At the Restoration of the monarchy in 1660 as much as possible was recovered and new regalia were made resembling the old.

Crowns. The earliest Sovereign's Crown now extant is the lineal successor of King Edward the Confessor's crown (hence its name St. Edward's Crown), and was made for the coronation of Charles II.

The earliest Queen's Crown was made for Mary of Modena, consort of James II.

The Imperial State Crown with two arches was made for the coronation of Queen Victoria in 1838. In it is set one ancient jewel, the ruby said to have been given to the Black Prince by Pedro the Cruel after the battle of Navarette, 1367, and later worn by Henry V in the coronet surrounding his helmet at the battle of Agincourt, 1415. The crown later had added to it the second largest of 'The Stars of Africa', cut from the Cullinan diamond, and altogether contains over 3,000 precious stones, mainly diamonds and pearls.

Set in the crown made in 1937 for the coronation of Queen Elizabeth the Queen Mother is the famous Indian diamond known as the Koh-i-noor.

The Prince of Wales's Crown has a single arch.

Orbs. The larger Orb was made for Charles II, the smaller for Mary II, consort of William III.

Sceptres. St. Edward's Staff, of gold, 4 ft. 7 in. long, is surmounted by an orb. The original was supposed to contain a fragment of the True Cross.

The Ampulla and Spoon   *The Imperial State Crown*   *The Exeter Salt*

The Royal Sceptre, surmounted by a cross, contains the largest of 'The Stars of Africa', cut from the Cullinan diamond. This is the biggest cut diamond in the world, weighing 530 carats.

The Sceptre with the dove is delivered into the Sovereign's left hand at the coronation.

The Queen's Sceptre with the cross was made for Mary of Modena.

The Queen's Sceptre with the dove was made for Mary II.

The Queen's ivory Rod, mounted in gold and enamelled, was also made for Mary of Modena.

Other Regalia. The pair of gold and enamelled Bracelets were made for Charles II, but were never used. The gold Armills which have replaced them were used at the coronation of Queen Elizabeth II.

The Gold Spurs of St. George were formerly buckled on as the emblems of chivalry. They are now touched by the Sovereign and placed on the Altar.

The Romanesque Anointing-spoon is one of the two ancient pieces which survive. It dates from the end of the twelfth century and was perhaps made for the coronation of John (1199–1216). The bowl of the spoon was restored for Charles II.

The ampulla, the vessel in the form of an eagle, which contains the oil for the anointing, is the other ancient piece, though not so old as the spoon. It dates in all probability from the time of Henry IV (1399–1413), but was restored for Charles II.

Plate. Besides the regalia proper, much royal plate is displayed, both

Yeoman Warders in Ceremonial Dress

ecclesiastical and secular. Some pieces have been used at coronations and other State occasions in the past; others are still so used. One fine piece of plate, 'Queen Elizabeth's Salt' dates from 1572–73: the remainder is practically all of the time of Charles II or William III and Mary II.

The Swords of State include the *Curtana* (without a point) denoting Mercy and the State Sword used at the opening of Parliament. Maces and trumpets are also displayed, some of them used at earlier coronations, and in the side cases are the insignia of the Orders of Knighthood, with their collars, stars and badges, and the highest of all decorations for valour, the Victoria Cross and the George Cross.

The Earliest Fortress

The Conqueror, before he entered London, ordered the construction of an advanced command post and, after his coronation at Christmas 1066, withdrew to Barking while the works were completed. The defended area was quite small, the south and east sides being formed by the river and the Roman city wall (repaired by King Alfred in 885), and the north and west sides by a newly dug ditch and rampart marked by the wall of the Inmost Ward. This wall was built within the early garrison-fort, the supervision of the work being entrusted to Gundulf, a monk of Bec in

The Bloody Tower (left) and the Wakefield Tower

Normandy who later became Bishop of Rochester. In 1097, under William Rufus, the works were still going on. A great storm in 1091 damaged the outworks. Ralf Flambard, Bishop of Durham, who was imprisoned in the Keep by Henry I, contrived to escape in 1101. During the wars between Stephen and Matilda, the Earl of Essex was Constable of the Tower, and even obtained a grant of the City of London. When he fell into Stephen's hands, the Tower formed the ransom, and the citizens regained their ancient Liberty. When Richard I was absent on the Crusade, his regent, Longchamp, resided in the Tower, of which he greatly enlarged the precincts by trespasses on the land of the City and of St. Katherine's Hospital. He surrendered the Tower to the citizens, led by Prince John, in 1191.

The whole Tower was held in pledge for the completion of Magna Carta in 1215 and 1216. At this time the Roman city wall and the river still formed the east and south sides of the castle, but a new ditch was dug and curtain wall built, extending to the defended area to the west. The new defences ran from the Roman city wall just north of the White Tower, across what is now the Parade Ground to the site of the later Beauchamp Tower. From there they turned southward to the river. The Bell Tower and the curtain wall between it and the Bloody Tower are all that survive of the defences of this time.

The White Tower or Keep

The White Tower, commenced by the Conqueror and completed by William Rufus, is the oldest visible part of the fortress and is one of the earliest and largest keeps in Western Europe. In plan it is somewhat irregular for although it looks so square from the river its four sides are all of different lengths, and three of its corners are not right-angles. The west side is 107 feet from north to south. The south side measures 118 feet. It has four turrets at the corners, three of them square, the fourth, that on the north-east, being circular. From floor to battlements it is 90 feet in height. The original entrance was on the south side, on the first floor, being reached, as usual in Norman castles, by an external staircase which has entirely disappeared. The interior is of the plainest and sternest character. Every consideration is subservient to that of obtaining the greatest strength and security. The outer walls vary in thickness from 15 feet in the lower to 11 feet in the upper storey. The whole building is crossed from north to south by one wall, which rises from base to summit and divides it into a larger western and a smaller eastern portion. The eastern part is further subdivided by a wall which cuts off the Chapel of St. John, its Crypt, and its Sub-crypt. There is a wooden floor between each end of the storeys of the other part.

The Tower and Tower Bridge from the Port of London Authority Building

View from Tower Bridge

The White Tower, or Keep

During the Middle Ages the Keep was truly the White Tower, thus in 1241 Henry III had the royal apartments in the Keep whitewashed, as well as the whole exterior. In addition he had the Chapel of St. John decorated with painting and stained glass.

During the wars with France, David, King of Scots, John, King of France, Charles of Blois, and John de Vienne, governor of Calais, and his twelve brave burgesses and many other illustrious prisoners were lodged here. In the Tower Richard II signed his abdication in 1399. The Duke of Orléans, taken at Agincourt, was lodged by Henry V in the White Tower. From that time the Beauchamp and other Towers were more used as prisons, but probably some of the Kentish rebels, taken with Wyatt in 1554, slept in the recesses of the Sub-crypt of the Chapel. In 1663 and later years down to 1709, structural repairs were carried out under the superintendence of Sir Christopher Wren, who replaced nearly all the Norman window openings with others of a classical character.

Near a staircase which has now disappeared, on the south side, some children's bones were found in the reign of Charles II. They were identified, somewhat conjecturally, with the remains of Edward V and his brother who disappeared so mysteriously at the accession of Richard III.

The Armouries: There has always been armour in the Tower of London. The present collection takes its shape from the reign of Henry VIII, to whose personal interest in the subject many of the present exhibits are due.

At that time the King's armour was distributed between the Tower and Greenwich, Westminster, Hampton Court and Windsor Castle. After the Restoration in 1660, when armour had fallen into disuse, Charles II had it concentrated in the Tower and at Windsor, and so, with few essential changes, it has remained.

The Armouries were a show place long before this and can claim to be the oldest museum in England. It was in Charles II's time that the historical line of kings was first set up, and this feature of the Armouries continued until well into the last century despite many anachronisms.

At various times additions have been and continue to be made, by transfer, gift and purchase, to the Armouries, increasing their scope as the national museum of European arms and armour. But the old Royal nucleus remains, and gives the Armouries a special character, binding them closely with the history of England.

There has been an unbroken succession of armed men within the walls of the Tower for nearly nine hundred years, at first wearing armour of mail, then of plate, and latterly in red coats and khaki.

The armour worn in the early Middle Ages was chiefly of mail, and consisted of a helmet, and a shirt and leggings constructed of riveted,

The Coronation Procession of Edward VI leaving the Tower in 1547

A German engraving showing Emperor Maximilian I visiting his armourers

interlinked iron rings; a shield was carried on the left arm. This was what William the Conqueror wore at Hastings, and Richard I and his Crusaders in Palestine. Their weapons were the lance and sword, and to a lesser degree the mace and axe. But mail, for all its flexibility, had certain disadvantages, and men began to reinforce it with pieces of plate. This process advanced rapidly during the fourteenth century, and the men-at-arms at Crécy and Poitiers wore a mixture of plate and mail. The advantage of plate armour lay in its glancing surface (like modern streamlining) and its unyielding resistance to a direct blow. The full harness of plate from head to foot, or 'white armour' as it was called, was finally evolved at the beginning of the fifteenth century, about the time of Agincourt. The best armour was made in Milan and in South Germany.

The introduction of gunpowder in the fourteenth century at first had little effect, except for siege purposes, and the musket did not finally oust the bow until the sixteenth century. Armour could be made thick enough to resist a bullet, but this greatly increased its weight. In the better organised armies of the sixteenth century, when freer tactical manoeuvring became possible, the heavily armoured horseman found himself at a disadvantage. But the knightly exercise of tilting still kept the armourers busy, and some of the finest craftsmen exercised their skill during this period.

When the English Civil War broke out in 1642 the day of defensive armour was almost over. Pikemen still continued to wear for a time half-armour, and the cavalry a helmet and a breast- and back-plate, or a coat of buff leather. Thereafter for nearly two centuries the weapon of offence was supreme, and regiments of the standing army were equipped in distinctive uniforms of cloth. In our own day armour has returned in the form of a tank, but with this difference, that it is, of course, mechanically propelled and encases several men instead of one.

Very little armour has survived from a time earlier than the fifteenth century. Mail was particularly liable to deterioration and was often cut up for other uses. Enriched armour of the sixteenth century usually owes its preservation to its intrinsic merits and personal associations; as exemplified here by four armours of Henry VIII, several of the Elizabethan courtiers, and of the Stuart princes. The armour of the common soldier had less chance of survival, and is, as a rule, found only in arsenals where numbers of retainers were kept. It is represented here by a few jacks and by troopers' and pikemen's armour of the seventeenth century.

Weapons of offence fall into four categories:

(1) The *arme blanche*, that is to say, the sword and dagger;
(2) Arms of percussion: the club, the mace, and the flail;
(3) Staff weapons (pole-arms): the lance, spear, pike and axe, and their relatives, the bill, halberd, partisan, etc.;
(4) Projectile weapons, which include:
(*a*) the long bow, crossbow, javelin and sling;
(*b*) firearms, *e.g.* the cannon and its diminutives, the hand gun (from which developed the musket and later the rifle) and the pistol.

It is worthy of remark that three modern principles in firearms were

Armour of Henry VIII for horse and man

Rare 'Gothic' armour of the late fifteenth century

Interior of the White Tower showing the massive cross wall that is part of the original structure

Grotesque helmet presented by the Emperor Maximilian I to King Henry VIII

understood early, namely, breech-loading, the rifled barrel and the revolving chamber, all of which can be seen here in specimens dating from the sixteenth and seventeenth centuries.

ARRANGEMENT OF THE ARMOURIES

English historical armour is set out in the Tudor Room (top floor); European armour in general in the Council Room (top floor); weapons of the first three categories in the Sword and Weapon Rooms (first floor); hand firearms up to 1700 in the Small Arms Room (ground floor); and ordnance in the vaults.

The visitor whose time is limited should allow enough to see the two rooms on the top floor, where the personal armours of the Kings of England are shown. On entering the White Tower the visitor finds himself on the ground floor of the building (known as the 'Gun Floor') used as a store for service arms between 1841 and 1916. The first room is known as

The Record Room: This contains two carved figures called 'Gin' and 'Beer', brought from the buttery of the Royal Palace of Greenwich at the end of the seventeenth century; the cloak in which General Wolfe died at Quebec in 1759; and portions of the state barge of the Master-General of the Ordnance. A model of the Tower is shown in this room. In one case are two daggers of Colonel Blood, who attempted to steal the Crown Jewels from the Tower in 1671.

Here, too, are the coat of the Duke of Wellington as Constable of the Tower and his sword and telescope. With them is an early sword of Napoleon Bonaparte.

In this and in the adjoining room are two of the original fireplaces.

At the southern end of this room is

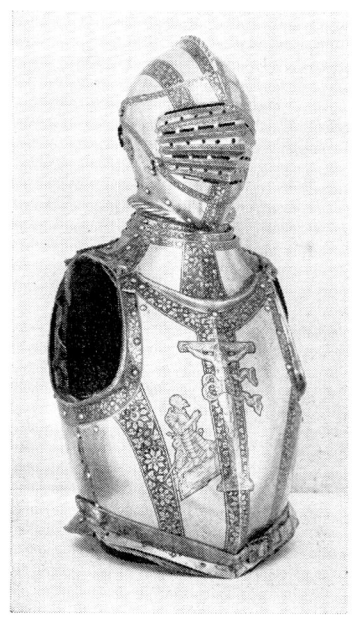

Armour with finely etched decoration—South German —c. 1550

Visored bascinet with mail aventail —Milanese—c. 1390

The Crypt of the Chapel of St. John: This contains several inscriptions carved by prisoners who took part in Wyatt's rebellion in 1554. Here are shown the block used at the execution of Simon, Lord Lovat, in 1747, the execution axe, dating from about 1660, some instruments of punishment, scythe-blades mounted as pole-arms used in Monmouth's rebellion, 1685, and a model of the rack.

From the Crypt the visitor passes westwards into

The Small Arms Room: The large opening in the south wall, now filled with glass, is the original entrance to the White Tower. Down the sides of the room are cases showing the development of firearms from the matchlock, through the wheel-lock to the flint-lock, and pistols of both types. Later weapons are to be seen in the New Armouries (*see page* 36).

With the matchlock, ignition of the charge of powder was made directly by a lighted 'match' or cord soaked in saltpetre. The wheel-lock depended on a piece of iron pyrites from which sparks were struck by a revolving wheel actuated by a spring, released by pressing the trigger. With the flint-lock, a piece of flint held in the jaws of the cock was made to strike sharply on a steel, and the spark so caused ignited the charge. The flint-lock remained in use for over two hundred years.

Some of the sporting guns with inlaid stocks, and pistols made in Brescia, are of exceptional quality. In the centre of the room is a mounted trooper of the period of the Civil War in England. Of the five richly decorated cannon, two were made for the Duke of Gloucester, son of Queen Anne, and two were taken from Paris in 1815, having belonged to Colbert, Minister of Finance to Louis XIV. The other gun, elaborately ornamented with laurel branches and medallions, mounted on a carriage carved to represent two Furies, was captured by the French at Malta in 1798. The ship which carried it to France was taken by the British frigate *Seahorse*, and with it was taken the banner of Baron Ferdinand Hompesch, last Grand Master of the Knights of Malta, which hangs near it.

From this room the visitor ascends by the staircase at the south-east angle and reaches the second floor of the tower, passing through the west doorway of

The Chapel of St. John: This takes up the south-east corner of this floor and of the floor above, and is of the greatest interest from its early date (*circa* 1080) and perfect condition. It is 55 feet 6 inches long by 31 feet wide, and has a nave and aisles of four bays and an apse opening by five arches to an ambulatory. The principal doorway is in the west bay of the north wall, and a second entrance opens from a wall passage at the south-west. The heavy round columns carry carved capitals, some of which bear a T-shaped figure found only at this early date. The arches are quite plain and above them is a clerestory lighted by a second tier of windows; its gallery is a continuation of the wall passages of the second floor. There are no old fittings in the Chapel; the glass in the windows was part of Horace Walpole's collection at Strawberry Hill. The altar hangings are made from cloth used for decorations at Westminster Abbey for the coronation of George VI.

The institution of the Order of the Bath was closely connected with this Chapel. Here Queen Mary I was betrothed to Count Egmont, proxy for Philip of Spain, in 1554.

Leaving the Chapel by the north door the visitor enters

The Sword Room: This contains cases devoted to swords illustrating the forms and varieties of this weapon from the early Middle Ages to the middle of the nineteenth century.

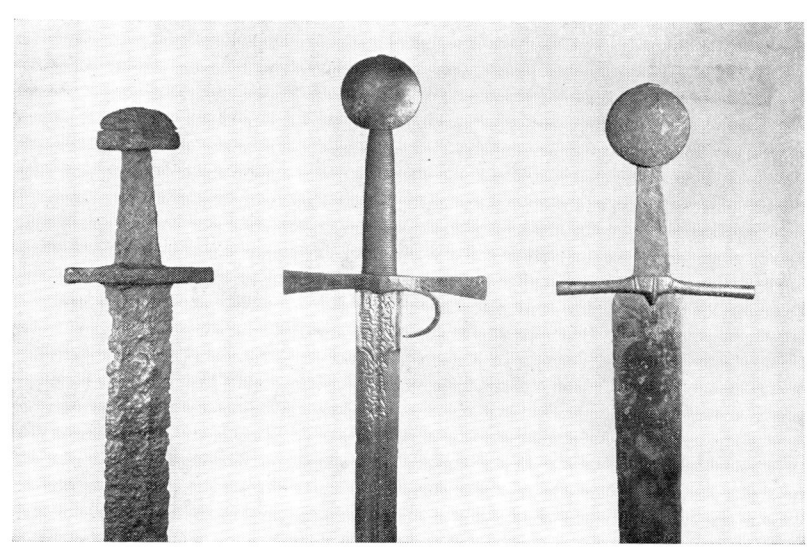

Medieval swords of the tenth to the fifteenth centuries

The sword of the Middle Ages was usually straight, double-edged, and had a simple cross-bar (quillons) to protect the hand. With the disuse of armour, the guard for the hand became more complicated. Different forms of rapier, small or court sword, and hunting swords are shown in this room and the next.

One case contains swords of George II, George III, George IV, William IV, Edward VII, George V and George VI, deposited by the Sovereign, and the sword of Frederick Augustus, Duke of York, deposited by George IV. The bows found in the wreck of the *Mary Rose*, 1545, are almost the only English long bows to have survived from ancient times.

Here will be noticed one of the original fireplaces of the White Tower, its flue being carried up for a short distance in the wall, and ending in narrow openings for the escape of smoke on either side of a buttress on the east face of the Tower. On this floor and on the floor below are small 'garderobe' chambers, or latrines, contrived in the thickness of the wall, some of them retaining the original arched vents on the outside. From this room opens

The Weapon Room: This was for many years known as the 'Banqueting

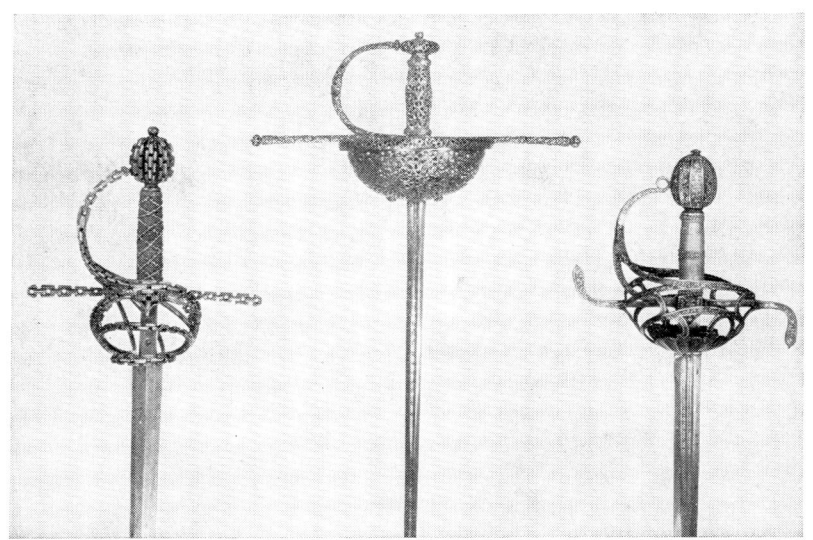

Rapiers of the sixteenth and seventeenth centuries

Room'. It contains specimens of staff weapons, maces, axes and other weapons of offence ranged round the room in stands, each labelled with the name of the type of weapon represented. At the south end of the room is a row of figures representing English pikemen.

The figures on horseback show one in armour of the knightly Gothic period about 1480—the horse armour, of great variety, came from the ducal family of Anhalt-Zerbst—and a cuirassier (heavy cavalry) of the Civil War period, when armour was last worn in the field.

On the wooden pillars are a number of breast- and back-plates stamped with the name 'Toiras', which were captured from Admiral de Toiras at the ill-fated siege of La Rochelle in 1627.

One case is devoted to the arms of the Scottish Highlands, the big two-handed sword or claymore, the basket-hilted broadsword, and the characteristic target (shield), guns, pistols and dirks.

Among the buff coats, which for a short time were substituted for body armour of iron, is one traditionally that of Colonel Francis Hacker, who supervised the execution of Charles I.

The staircase at the north-west angle, facing the parade ground, gives access to

The Horse Armoury: This was originally the Council Chamber, and has witnessed many memorable scenes in the history of this country. The armoured figures, horse and foot, up the centre and ranged in order along the party-wall, show the development of armour from the late fifteenth century to the reign of Charles I. 'Gothic' armour of the fifteenth century is of great rarity and admired for its graceful lines.

In one table case and one wall case are shown examples of the complicated fabric of mail, which preceded 'white' plain armour, but continued to be used as an accessory.

The group of figures, mounted and on foot, at the rear of the procession are wearing armour specially designed for the tournament. That in front is one of a series of tilt-armours made for the Emperor Maximilian I, the

Armour of Henry VIII made at Greenwich c. 1535

Tonlet (skirted) armour of Henry VIII, Milanese, c. 1510

German tilt-armour c. 1590 with lance

30

ally of Henry VIII, who styled himself 'the last of the knights'. Tilt-armours are generally heavier and less mobile than field (war) armours.

In these contests the opponents passed left arm to left arm and the lance was always pointed to the adversary's left side. It was therefore of the highest importance that armour, besides being of strong material, should present as much as possible a glancing surface to the weapon, whether sword, mace, or lance.

Arranged in cases is a series of helmets, which range from a rare visored bascinet of the fourteenth century, from the Castle of Churburg, and sallets of the fifteenth, to the close-helmets, morions and pots of later years. Note the massive *Brocas* tilting helm. Other cases show armour of

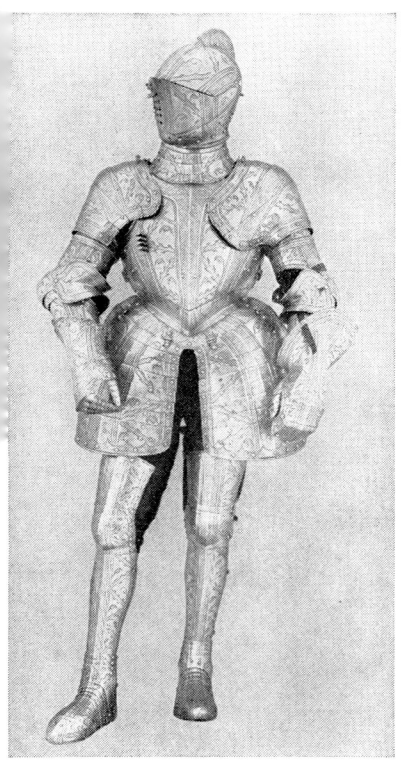

Armour of Robert Dudley, Earl of Leicester, made at Greenwich, c. 1585

Cromwellian pikeman

Close helmet, embossed and damascened with gold and silver, of the 'Lion' armour presented to Henry Prince of Wales

the Christian garrison at Rhodes before its capture by the Turks in 1523, and some enriched armours of the sixteenth century.

The Tudor Room: All the exhibits in this room are connected with the history of England. Much of the armour shown here was made in the Royal workshops at Greenwich, established by Henry VIII for his own use. The King's harness for fighting on foot is an early work of the Greenwich shops and weighs 93 lb. Another with deep skirt or *tonlet* was only recently completed when the missing legs were found, after a lapse of three centuries, at the home of the King's Champion in Lincolnshire. The quaint helmet

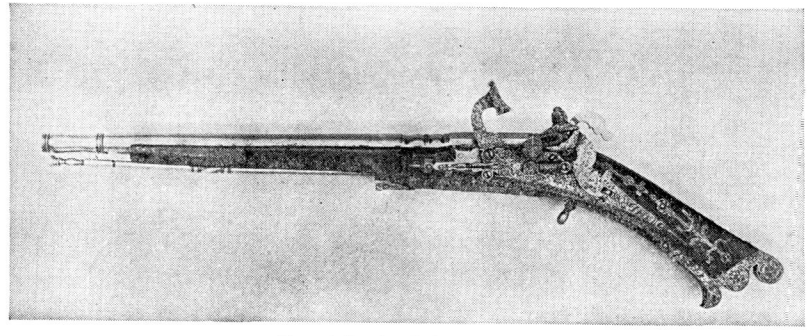

Scottish pistol dated 1619

*Close helmet
of William Somerset,
3rd Earl of Worcester,
made in the Royal Workshops
at Greenwich c. 1570-80*

with the ram's horns on it, the *Burgundian* bard for a horse, and the body armour on the mounted figure nearby were all presented to Henry VIII by the Emperor Maximilian. The other complete armour for man and horse was made for the King in later life when he was big and heavy. The spiked club with three pistol-barrels in the head was known as 'Henry VIII's Walking Staff'. Note the lance of immense size, known as that of Charles Brandon, Duke of Suffolk, the boon companion of Henry VIII. It was seen here and recorded by Hentzner in his travels in 1598. In the cases along the party-walls are the Greenwich-made armours of Queen Elizabeth's favourite, Robert Dudley, Earl of Leicester (em-

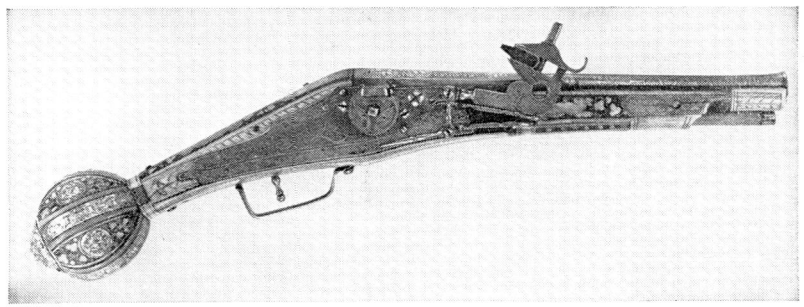

Wheel-lock pistol—German—c. 1580

bossed with the bear and ragged staff), and other prominent Elizabethans, Sir John Smythe, the soldier and diplomat, and Lord Worcester, whose company of players included Shakespeare. Near the exit are an armour for a man of about 6 feet 10 inches in height traditionally (but erroneously) known as 'John of Gaunt', and a richly embossed and damascened armour decorated with lions' masks.

The large case on the end wall shows the gilt armour of Charles I presented to him by the City of London (the face of the King was carved by Grinling Gibbons), boy's armour of Charles II when Prince, and that of James II, made when armour was falling into disuse.

The visitor leaves the Tudor Room by the north-east stairway and descends to the basement popularly called the 'dungeons', which, in spite of the romantic tales of prisoners drowned at high tide, is more than 10 feet above high water mark. It was vaulted in brick about 1730, and is divided into three rooms, of which that entered from the stair is known as

The Mortar Room: Here are shown the bronze mortars, formerly placed in the Gun Park, with other pieces of ordnance. At the south end is a mortar of nine bores used for fireworks at the peace of Aix-la-Chapelle in 1748. Near to this is a ship's gun dredged from the wreck of H.M.S. *Royal George*, sunk by accident in 1782—Admiral Kempenfeldt and the whole crew of over six hundred men were drowned in that disaster. To the left of this is a large mortar used at the siege of Namur in 1794, and fired so frequently that the touch hole or vent became fused with the heat. The carriage was burnt away in the fire of 1841, leaving only the framework of iron, which was filled up with wood at a later period. To the right are French mortars and in the wall is a carved stone panel of the Lion of St. Mark brought from Corfu in 1809. Near the staircase are stone shot of the sixteenth century. Round the walls are muskets, rifles and wall-pieces.

At the south end of the Mortar Room is the sub-Crypt of the Chapel of St. John. The passage through the thickness of the wall giving access to this chamber was once a small cell sometimes used for the confinement of prisoners and known as the Little Ease. The Sub-crypt, which has a barrel vault and was dimly lighted from the east, may have been occasionally used for keeping prisoners, but was normally a store room.

In the west wall is an opening cut in the eighteenth century, when the basement was used as a powder store. It gives access to

The Cannon Room: At the north end are iron guns of the early sixteenth century, including some interesting pieces dredged from the wreck of the *Mary Rose*, sunk in action with the French in 1545. Near these are bronze guns made for Henry VIII, and in the bays between the piers are placed

The Cannon Room in the vaults of the White Tower. The cannons are of the sixteenth and seventeenth centuries. The armour and pikes are part of the stores preserved in the Tower of London since the Civil War.

selected examples of English and foreign guns which were formerly exhibited in the Gun Park on the west side of the White Tower. The Well on the east side dates from the twelfth century and is 40 feet deep. When it was cleaned out in 1910 the wooden frame on which its stones were built was found in place at the bottom.

With this room the tour of the White Tower is completed.

The Parade

This is the open space between the Waterloo Barracks on the north and the White Tower on the south. The Barracks were built in 1845 on the site of the Great Storehouse burnt in 1841. The building of similar character to the right contains the Regimental Headquarters and Museum of the Royal Fusiliers (City of London Regiment).

The Royal Fusiliers Museum

This contains relics and trophies dating from the formation of the regiment in 1685 to the present day, and a fine display of silver and china. Uniforms include those worn by George V as Colonel-in-Chief, and the collection of medals contains three Victoria Crosses. Dioramas depict the battles of Albuera (1811), Alma (1854), Mons (1914), and Cassino (1944), in which the Royal Fusiliers played a distinguished part.

The New Armouries

This late seventeenth-century building of red brick with two projecting wings has recently been restored to its original purpose to form an addition to the armouries in the White Tower, and covers the eighteenth and nineteenth centuries. On the entrance floor is a representative collection of Oriental armour and weapons intended for comparison with the European, the centre of the room being dominated by an Indian armour for an elephant once the property of the first Lord Clive and probably a trophy from the battle of Plassey in 1757.

On the first floor are firearms both for war and for sporting purposes, many of them of the finest quality. They include one with a silver barrel presented by Louis XIV to the first Duke of Richmond, and a garniture made for the Empress Elizabeth of Russia, examples of the work of Manton and Boutet; and a series of British service muskets and rifles from the late seventeenth century to 1914. Notice too the examples of the work of the Rev. Alexander Forsyth, who invented the percussion system of ignition when working inside the Tower. Napoleon I offered him for his secret £20,000 which he declined. On this floor also is the Students' Room containing a large collection of firearms of all countries, showing the

The Royal Chapel of St. Peter ad Vincula—early sixteenth century

development of breech and ignition mechanisms. It can be seen on written application to the Master of the Armouries.

On the second floor is a collection of objects of military interest, including a group of early machine-guns.

The Royal Chapel of St. Peter ad Vincula

This is so called from having been consecrated on that well-known festival of the Latin Church, August 1st, probably in the reign of Henry I (1100–35). The chapel was rebuilt at the end of the thirteenth century. It was burnt in 1512 and almost entirely rebuilt, and has since then undergone a great deal of repair. (*For admission apply to Yeoman Warder.*) In the memorable words of Stow, writing in the reign of Queen Elizabeth I, there lie before the high altar 'two dukes between two queens, to wit, the Duke of Somerset and the Duke of Northumberland, between Queen Anne and Queen Katharine, all four beheaded'. Here also are buried Lady Jane Grey and Lord Guildford Dudley, the Duke of Monmouth, and the Scottish lords, Kilmarnock, Balmerino, and Lovat, beheaded for their share in the rebellion of 1745. The last burial in the chapel was that of

Charles Wyndham, Keeper of the Regalia, in 1872; the canopied tomb of John Holland, Duke of Exeter and Constable of the Tower, who died in 1447, was brought here in 1951, having been previously moved from its original position in St. Katherine's Hospital by the Tower in 1827. The altar frontal is of cloth used for coronation decorations in Westminster Abbey in 1937 and 1953.

Tower Green

The space south of the chapel is so called, and was used as a burial ground; in the middle is a small square plot paved with granite, showing the site on which stood at rare intervals the scaffold for private executions. It was paved by order of Queen Victoria. The following persons are known to have been executed on or near this spot:

1. William, Lord Hastings, by order of Richard, Duke of Gloucester, in June, 1483.
2. Queen Anne Boleyn, second wife of Henry VIII, May 19th, 1536.
3. Margaret, Countess of Salisbury, the last of the old Angevin or Plantagenet family, May 27th, 1541.
4. Queen Katharine Howard, fifth wife of Henry VIII, February 13th, 1542.

A tournament at Smithfield before Edward IV and the King of France in 1467

The Queen's House

5. Jane, Viscountess Rochford, February 13th, 1542.
6. Lady Jane Grey, wife of Lord Guildford Dudley, February 12th, 1554.
7. Robert Devereux, Earl of Essex, February 25th, 1601.

They were all beheaded with an axe except Queen Anne Boleyn, whose head was cut off with a sword by an executioner brought over from St. Omer. The bodies of all seven were buried in the Chapel of St. Peter.

The Beauchamp Tower

This is on the west side of Tower Green, facing the White Tower, and is on the inner wall between the Bell Tower on the south and the Devereux Tower on the north, being connected with both by a walk along the wall-top. Its present name probably refers to the residence in it, as a prisoner, of Thomas, third Earl of Warwick, of the Beauchamp family, who was attainted under Richard II in 1397, but restored to his honours and liberty two years later under Henry IV. It is curious that the most interesting associations of the place should be with his successors in the earldom. Although built entirely for defensive purposes, we find it thus early used as a prison, and during the two following centuries it seems to have been

*Prisoners' inscriptions on the walls of the Beauchamp Tower:
Left, T. Salmon, 1622; centre, the Dudley Brothers, 1553;
right, G. Gifford, 1586*

regarded as one of the most convenient places in which to lodge prisoners of rank; in consequence many of the most interesting mural inscriptions are to be found in its chambers.

In plan the Beachamp Tower is semicircular, and it projects 18 feet beyond the face of the wall. It consists of three storeys, of which the middle one is on a level with the rampart, on which it formerly opened. The building dates from the reign of Edward I, though on the line of Richard I's defences; the brickwork is of the time of Henry VIII. It is entered at the south-east corner and a circular staircase ascends to the middle chamber, which is spacious and has a large window and a fireplace. Here are to be found most of the inscriptions, some having been brought from other chambers. A few are in the entrance passage and on the stairs. All are numbered and catalogued. The following—to which the numbers are appended—will be found the most interesting:

On the ground floor, near the entrance, ROBART DVDLEY (2). This was the fifth son of John, Duke of Northumberland, and next brother to Guildford Dudley, the husband of Lady Jane Grey. When his father was brought to the block in 1553 he and his brother remained in prison here, Robert being condemned to death in 1554. In the following year he was liberated with his elder brother, Ambrose, afterwards created Earl of Warwick, and his younger brother, Henry. In the first year of Queen Elizabeth I he was made Master of the Horse and chosen a Knight of the Garter. In 1564 he was created Earl of Leicester. He died at Cornbury, in Oxfordshire, in 1588.

On the left, at the entrance of the great chamber, is a carved cross, with

Armoury in the White Tower

Tower Wharf, with St. Thomas's Tower and Traitors' Gate

Yeoman Warders on parade at the installation of a Constable

other religious emblems, with the name and arms of PEVEREL, and the date 1570 (8). It is supposed to have been cut by a Roman Catholic prisoner confined in the reign of Elizabeth I.

Over the fireplace this inscription in Latin: 'The more suffering for Christ in this world the more glory with Christ in the next', etc. (13). This is signed 'Arundel, June 22, 1587'. This was Philip Howard, son of Thomas, Duke of Norfolk, beheaded in 1572. Philip inherited from his maternal grandfather the Earldom of Arundel in 1580. He was a staunch Roman Catholic and was constantly under suspicion of the Government, by which in 1584 he was confined in his own house for a short time. On his liberation he determined to quit the country, but was committed to the Tower in 1585, and died in custody ten years later, having refused release on condition of forsaking his religion. His body was buried in his father's grave in the Chapel of St. Peter, but was eventually removed to Arundel. He left other inscriptions, one in the window (79), and one on the staircase (91), dated 1587.

On the right of the fireplace is an elaborate piece of sculpture (14), which will be examined with peculiar interest as a memorial of the five brothers Dudley: Ambrose (created Earl of Warwick 1561), Guildford (beheaded 1554), Robert (created Earl of Leicester 1564), and Henry (killed at the siege of St. Quentin, 1557), carved by the eldest, John (called Earl of Warwick), who died in 1554. Under a bear and a lion supporting a ragged staff is the name of 'JOHN DVDLE' and surrounding them is a wreath of roses (for Ambrose), oak leaves (for Robert, *robur*, an oak), gillyflowers (for Guildford), and honeysuckle (for Henry). Below are four lines, one of them incomplete, alluding to the device and its meaning. It is on record that the Lieutenant of the Tower was allowed 6s. 8d. a day each for the diet of these captive brothers.

No. 33 is one of several incriptions relating to the Poole or Pole family. (*See also* Nos. 45, 47, 52, 56, 57.) They were the grandsons of the Countess of Salisbury, who was beheaded in 1541. No. 45 contains the name of 'GEFFRYE POOLE 1562'. He was the second son, and he gave evidence against his elder brother, Lord Montagu, who was beheaded in 1539.

'IANE' (48). This interesting inscription, repeated also in the window (85), has always been supposed to refer to Lady Jane Grey, daughter of the Duke of Suffolk and wife of Guildford Dudley, fourth son of the Duke of Northumberland. A second repetition in another part of the room was unfortunately obliterated in the last century when a new window was made to fit this chamber for a mess-room. It is sometimes, but erroneously, supposed that the name was carved by this Queen of ten days herself, but it is improbable that she was ever imprisoned in the Beauchamp Tower.

St. John's Chapel in the White Tower—c. 1080

*Decorated capital
in St. John's Chapel*

She is known to have lived in the house of Partridge, the Gaoler. It is much more probable that the two inscriptions were placed on the wall either by Lord Guildford Dudley, her husband, or by his brother, whose large device has been described above (14)

In the window is the rebus, or monogram, of Thomas Abell (66); upon a bell is the letter A. This was Dr. Abell, a faithful servant to Queen Katharine of Aragon, first wife of Henry VIII. He acted as her chaplain during the progress of the divorce, and by his determined advocacy offended the King. For denying Royal supremacy in the Church he was condemned and executed in 1540. There are many other records of this kind in the Beauchamp Tower

On leaving Beauchamp Tower and turning to the right the visitor sees, facing Tower Green,

The Queen's House

Until about 1880 this was called The Lieutenant's Lodgings. The present house was built in about 1530 and may have replaced the medieval constable's house. It is a good example of a timber-framed house and originally contained a spacious hall two storeys in height. A floor was later inserted in the upper part of the hall and the resultant room became known as the Council Chamber. It contains an elaborate contemporary memorial

SOME FAMOUS

Robert Dudley, Earl of Leicester, 1532–1588

Queen Elizabeth I 1533–1603

Sir Walter Raleigh, 1552–1618

tablet of the Gunpowder Plot—it was in this room that the interrogation of the conspirators took place. In the north wing is the small room where Anne Boleyn spent the last days of her life. On the west side is the rampart known as Elizabeth's Walk. The doorway is that through which in 1716 Lord Nithsdale escaped in female attire the evening before he was to have been beheaded. As a result of the ill-starred Stuart rebellion of 1715,

Queen Anne Boleyn, 1507–1536

Judge Jeffreys, 1648–1689

Margaret, Countess of Salisbury, 1473–1541

TOWER PRISONERS

Robert Devereux, Earl of Essex, 1566–1601

Simon Fraser, Lord Lovat, 1667–1747

St. Thomas More, 1478–1535

Nithsdale and six other Scottish nobles were brought up to London and paraded through the streets to prison. They were tried in February, 1716, and condemned to death. Three were later pardoned. Nithsdale's young wife had braved snowbound roads all the way from their home in Dumfriesshire to plead for his life. When that failed, she persuaded a woman friend to put on two dresses and go with her to the condemned cell—where

Lord Nithsdale, 1676–1744

Thomas Cromwell, Earl of Essex, 1485–1540

James, Duke of Monmouth, 1649–1685

*Aisle in
St. John's Chapel*

Rampart south of Beauchamp Tower, known as Elizabeth's Walk

Nithsdale donned the spare dress and made good his escape, eventually travelling to Rome disguised, this time as one of the footmen of the Venetian ambassador.

The interior of the Queen's House is not shown to the public. Next to it is the house of the Yeoman Gaoler. It was in this house that Lady Jane Grey lived when a prisoner, and from its windows saw her husband go forth from the adjoining Beauchamp Tower to his execution on Tower Hill and his headless body brought to the Chapel 'in a carre', while on the green in front, the scaffold was being prepared for her own execution on the same day, Monday, February 12th, 1554.

The Salt Tower

(*For admission to this Tower and the Martin Tower described below, please apply in writing to the Resident Governor.*)

This was formerly called Julius Caesar's Tower and is of special interest as containing more prisoners' inscriptions than any other, except the Beauchamp Tower; they are, moreover, in their original places, while many of those in the Beauchamp Tower are not. Among them the most conspicuous is the figure for casting horoscopes cut by Hew Draper of Bristol in 1561. He was sent to the Tower for an accusation of witchcraft against Lady St. Lo, better known as Bess of Hardwick, and her husband Sir William St. Lo. A finely cut armillary sphere is also to be seen, and a pierced heart, hand and foot occur in different places on the wall, signifying

Cannon on the river front

the five wounds of Christ. The name of Michael Moody, 1587, recalls a plot to murder Elizabeth I, and here as in the other tower are several inscriptions marked by the IHS monogram, with a cross above the H, a form commonly used by members of the Society of Jesus.

The Martin Tower

This is of Henry III's time though it has been much cut about and modernised. It had originally a single room on each floor, and remains of embrasures and the large stone fireplaces are to be seen. There are a number of prisoners' inscriptions, mostly of the early seventeenth century, about the time of the Gunpowder Plot. This tower was formerly inhabited by the Keeper of the Regalia, and was the scene of the attempt by Colonel Blood in 1671 to steal the State Crown and other regalia. Having first spied out the land in clerical disguise, and ingratiated himself with the old keeper, Talbot Edwards, Blood came back with two accomplices, all being armed with pistols, swordsticks and daggers. Leaving poor Edwards for dead (in fact, he died a few years afterwards), Blood hid the Crown under his cloak, while one companion put the Orb in his breeches pocket,

The Wharf with the Lanthorn Tower and Cradle Tower in the background

and the other started filing the Sceptre in half to carry away. At this point they were disturbed by Edwards's son; and in the running fight that followed, Blood and his companions were captured.

Blood's enigmatic remark that 'it was a brave attempt, for it was for a crown', coupled with the fact that Charles II not only pardoned him forthwith, but conferred a pension and certain Irish estates on him, led some to suppose either that Charles, in need of money, had commissioned Blood to steal the treasures, or that Blood knew some awkward secrets about the King.

The Martin Tower was damaged by bomb-blast in the last war.

Bastion of the Roman London Wall

The remains of the medieval Wardrobe Tower incorporate the base of a Roman tower of U-shaped plan and apparently hollow. This base of rubble masonry with a double bonding course of tiles set in pink mortar stands to a height of 5 feet. The large-gritted buff mortar of the Roman rubble work is quite distinct from the whitish mortar of the medieval reconstruction. There is also a 10-foot length of wall standing to a height of

Firing a Royal Salute

nearly 5 feet at the back of the Wardrobe Tower. The line of this fragment, if produced southwards, would strike the Lanthorn Tower (*see plan*).

North Front

On the outer circuit of wall at the north-west and north-east angles are two bastions added by Henry VIII, known as Legge's Mount and Brass Mount respectively. There was a similar bastion at the north angle, added in the reign of Queen Victoria at the time of the Chartist riots—the last addition to the fortifications of the Tower. Its destruction by a German bomb on October 5th, 1940, revealed the original line of the Curtain Wall, which has now been rebuilt instead of the bastion. Two other buildings of the Tower were destroyed by enemy bombs, the modern Main Guard between the Wakefield and White Towers (December 29th, 1940—*see page* 14), and the north end of the late eighteenth-century 'Hospital Block', to the east of the White Tower (September 22nd, 1940), now rebuilt.

River Front and Wharf

East of St. Thomas's Tower two further towers should be noted on the outer curtain. The Cradle Tower is a fourteenth-century water-gate with a contemporary vault similar to that in the gate-passage beneath the Bloody Tower, but the present upper part of the tower dates from the nineteenth century. Further to the east and beyond a modern entrance through the curtain, the Well Tower also has an original vault of the time of Henry III.

The Wharf itself in its present form is relatively recent, but evidence for a wharf at the Tower of London goes back to the early fourteenth century, and by the end of that century a stone wharf stretched along practically the whole of the river frontage of the Tower.

Here may be seen a number of guns of historic interest from many parts of the world; the more important bear their dates and histories on brass plates.

Tradition at the Tower

Among events of tradition and pageantry that take place at the Tower the following should be mentioned, one occurring daily, one frequently, and two at regular intervals:

The Ceremony of the Keys

A ceremony centuries old is enacted every night at 10 p.m. when the main gates of the Tower are locked. Five minutes before the hour the Chief Yeoman Warder joins an escort consisting of a sergeant and three men who are detailed to help him close the three gates. When the keys return, the sentry calls a challenge: 'Halt, who goes there?' The Chief Warder replies: 'The keys.' The exchange continues with 'Whose keys?'— 'Queen Elizabeth's keys.' Then the guard present arms: the Chief Warder, doffing his Tudor bonnet, calls: 'God preserve Queen Elizabeth'; and the whole guard respond: 'Amen.' The keys are finally carried by the Chief Warder to the Queen's House where they are secured for the night.

Royal Salutes

The Governor of the Tower has the duty of giving notice in writing to the Honourable Artillery Company that a Royal Salute is due to be fired from the Tower on a particular day. For a great State event the proper salute is 62 guns; likewise for the anniversary of the Sovereign's birth, accession, or coronation. When Parliament is opened by the Sovereign in person the appropriate salute is 41 guns; it is the same for the birth of a Royal infant. A detachment of the Honourable Artillery Company take four guns to the Tower, setting them up in the Gun Park in the forenoon; the salute having been discharged, the guns are returned on the same day.

The Execution Block and Axe

Beating the Bounds

In Anglo-Saxon times it was the boys who were beaten at parish boundaries so that they were made sure of remembering them; nowadays the boys give instead of receiving a beating. Every third year at Rogationtide the bounds of the Tower Liberty are beaten by choirboys of the Royal Chapel and children dwelling within the Tower. After a service in St. Peter ad Vincula a procession is formed by the Governor, Chaplain, Warders, residents, and choir, the children carrying white wands. There are 31 boundary stones, and at each of them the Chaplain proclaims: 'Cursed is he who removeth his neighbour's landmark', and the Chief Warder urges the beaters on with: 'Whack it, boys, whack it.'

Installation of the Constable

The office of Constable of the Tower has existed almost since the Norman Conquest, for William I made the first appointment about 1078 to reward Geoffrey de Mandeville for good service at Hastings and elsewhere. Always regarded as an office of honour and dignity—in the Middle Ages, of profit also—it is held by Royal Letters Patent under the Great Seal and confers the privilege of audience and direct communication with the Sovereign. In 1933 the tenure was altered from life to five years. A long line of distinguished prelates, soldiers, and statesmen who have been Constable includes William Longchamp, Bishop of Ely; Walter de Stapledon, Bishop of Exeter; the Duke of Wellington, from 1826 to 1852 (since when every Constable has been a soldier); Lord Napier of Magdala;

Choirboys of St. Peter ad Vincula beating the bounds

Lord Wavell; Lord Alanbrooke; Lord Wilson of Libya; and since 1965 Field-Marshal Sir Gerald Templer.

When a new Constable is installed a traditional ceremony is carried out on Tower Green. The Yeoman Warders, a body appointed by Henry VII, form up in a circle, while a detachment of troops and trumpeters are in attendance. The Lord Chamberlain arrives at the steps near the Bloody Tower and proceeds to the Queen's House, where the keys are handed to him by the Lieutenant of the Tower. The Sovereign's proclamation that the new incumbent shall 'have, hold, exercise, and enjoy' his functions having been read by the Lieutenant, the keys are delivered to him by the Lord Chamberlain, whereupon the Chief Warder cries: 'God preserve Queen Elizabeth', and all the Warders respond: 'Amen.' The new Constable inaugurates his office by carrying out an inspection of the Warders and troops on parade.

The Ravens

Ravens were once common in London's streets and were protected for the services they rendered as scavengers. It is probable that there have always been ravens at the Tower, and there is a legend that the Tower will fall if its loses its ravens. The birds are therefore carefully guarded. Six are kept 'on the establishment' and are cared for by a Yeoman Warder who is the Yeoman Quartermaster.

Each bird receives a weekly allowance of 3s. worth of horseflesh. They have their own quarters in a cage by the Lanthorn Tower.

Before their wings were clipped ravens have wandered from the Tower, and there was one that used to fly off to perch on St. Paul's Cathedral. In the winter of 1889–90 a bird, probably this same one, took up residence in Kensington Gardens.

Ravens can attain a good age, and one of the Tower birds, James Crow, was a resident for 44 years. The birds are not popular with everyone, they are often noisy, and will amuse themselves by removing putty from windows, causing damage to unattended cars, and taking sly pecks at ladies' legs!

Ravens on Tower Green

Acknowledgments

The portrait of Lord Nithsdale is reproduced by courtesy of the Trustees of the Scottish National Portrait Gallery.

All the other portraits on pages 44 and 45 are reproduced by courtesy of the Trustees of the National Portrait Gallery, London.

The picture of the Royal Mint on page 11 is from an engraving in the Guildhall Library.

The print of the Byward Tower on page 6 is reproduced by courtesy of the Trustees of the British Museum.

The print of the Royal Menagerie on page 5 was kindly supplied by Mr. Noël Hume.

General Information

Photography, Sketching. Exteriors of buildings: no pass required. Interiors of Chapels Royal, Beauchamp, and Bloody Towers*, and Armouries†: passes required.

* To be obtained beforehand from the Constable's office. (01-709 0765.)
† To be obtained from the Master of the Armouries, White Tower, Tower of London, E.C.3 (01-709 0765) Passes not required for hand cameras in the White Tower and New Armouries.

Guides. Yeoman Warder Guides, if available, can be obtained at Byward Tower.

Restaurant. Open to the public on days when the Tower is open to visitors from 10 a.m. to 6 p.m. in summer; from 10 a.m. to 5 p.m. in winter.

Wharf front. Open, admission free, through East and West Gates. Weekdays: 7 a.m. to sunset. Sundays: 10 a.m. to sunset.

Transport

Railways. Liverpool Street Station, $\frac{3}{4}$ mile (78 bus). London Bridge Station, $\frac{1}{2}$ mile (47 bus to Tower Bridge Road, then 6 minutes' walk or 42 or 78 bus).

Buses. 42, 78, or any bus crossing London Bridge.

Green Line Coaches. Minories Coach Station, $\frac{1}{4}$ mile (42 or 78 bus).

Underground. Tower Hill Station (Inner Circle or District), 2 minutes' walk.

SEASON TICKETS

Season tickets, valid for a year, admit their holders to all the ancient monuments and historic buildings in the care of the Ministry of Public Building and Works. They can be obtained by writing to the Ministry (C.I.O. Branch), Lambeth Bridge House, London, S.E.1; at H.M.S.O. bookshops listed on the back cover; or at most monuments.

Printed in England for Her Majesty's Stationery Office by The Thanet Press, Margate
Cover by A. Wheaton & Co. Ltd., Exeter.   Dd. 153157 K 3624 7/69